I0122661

HEAVENLY ANGEL LAY LAY

EXPLAINS WHY

PROFESSIONAL

COUNSELORS

HAVE

'HARDENED

HEARTS'

PUBLISHING COMPANY

ISBN: 978-0-6151-7482-2

www.crossover-ministries-publishing.com

TABLE OF CONTENTS

1. About the Author   4
2. Introduction   5

A 'HARDENED HEART'

3. Straighten Out the Heart   7

ISAAC AND REBEKAH

5. Isaac and Rebekah continued   18

BIBLIOGRAPHY

6. Bibliography   48

ABOUT THE AUTHOR

I was dedicated to Jesus Christ of Nazareth as an infant and accepted Him as my Lord and Savior around seven years old when a visiting youth group led me in prayer at the alter. During my Salvation Prayer I asked Jesus to use me in a special ministry. Something that very few other Christians would want to do. I saw all the people just sitting in the pews, the ushers, and the Sunday School teachers and realized any Christian could do that. I wanted something different. One day in church service there was a visiting minister at a church I was visiting as well. The Minister said, "Jesus is going to make you a 'Healer of a Heart'". Then he asked me if I knew what that meant. I said, "No." the minister said, "I don't either, but whatever it is, Jesus is going to use you in a powerful way.

Helping Rachael, Jesus showed me what a 'Healer of the Heart' is. During the course of me helping Rachael to the 'Promised Land', a real Heavenly Angel named Lay Lay and I were allowed one hour one day to talk about Spiritual and Family situations from the King James Version of the Word of God. These books are designed to answer a lot of Spiritual Questions not even your minister can answer or your Church Denomination. I know theology Doctors who can't tell you how people other than Noah and his family made it past the 'Great Flood', yet their names are listed in the King James Version of the Word of God right after the 'World Wide Flood'. These books explain that and much more. I have written these books to tell the whole truth about the Word of God no matter how difficult it may be for me or others. Yes, there are things I write in these books that I don't even like, but in all fairness and total honestly, I must say the WHOLE TRUTH. The title of this book is 100% real. HEAVENLY ANGEL LAY LAY explained to me how a person comes to get a 'Hardened Heart', what a 'Hardened Heart' is and how to recover from a 'Hardened Heart'.

INTRODUCTION

The first section of this book talks about the **HARDENED HEART** of all humans, but particularly **Professionals in Authoritative Positions**. How their Hearts became Hardened to begin with and what can be done about the pain and anger still within their hearts, how their Hardened Heart influences their decisions in their Authoritative Positions and the consequences of their decisions on the lives of others they have influence over. The second section of this book contains the good and bad times of Isaac and Rebekah as a couple. All scriptures are taken from the King James Version of the Word of God. This book contains an excerpt from my book. MATTHEW'S WORD 'TWO':REAL WORD OF GOD BIBLE.

BOOKS WRITTEN BY WALTER BURCHETT, BA:

MATTHEW'S WORD 'TWO':REAL WORD OF GOD BIBLE   ISBN: 1-4116-6995-9

HEAVENLY ANGEL LAY LAY EXPLAINS WHY ADAM WAS NEVER CURSED
                                                          ISBN: 978-1-84728-176-0

HEAVENLY ANGEL LAY LAY EXPLAINS WHY ABORTED BABIES DO NOT GO TO HEAVEN
                                                          ISBN: 978-0-6151-7470-9

HEAVENLY ANGEL LAY LAY EXPLAINS THE BIBLICAL GROUNDS FOR MARRIAGE,
        SEPARATION, AND DIVORCE   ISBN: 978-0-6151-7481-5

HEAVENLY ANGEL LAY LAY EXPLAINS WHY PROFESSIONAL COUNSELORS HAVE 'HARDENED
        HEARTS'   ISBN: 978-0-6151-7482-2

HEAVENLY ANGEL LAY LAY EXPLAINS THE DIFFERENCE BETWEEN A 'COLD CHRISTIAN' AND
        A 'BACKSLIDER'   ISBN: 978-0-6151-7483-9

HEAVENLY ANGEL LAY LAY EXPLAINS WHICH BIBLE TO READ, WHICH BIBLE NOT TO READ,
        AND WHY   ISBN: 978-0-6151-7484-6

HEAVENLY ANGEL LAY LAY EXPLAINS WHY GAYS, LESBIANS, BI-SEXUALS, AND
        TRANSSEXUALS DO NOT GO TO HEAVEN   ISBN: 978-0-6151-7485-3

HEAVENLY ANGEL LAY LAY EXPLAINS WHY CHILDREN AND SPORTS ARE DEFINITELY A
        RELIGION IN TODAY'S SOCIETY   ISBN: 978-0-6151-7486-0

HEAVENLY ANGEL LAY LAY EXPLAINS WHAT 'MANY ARE CALLED, BUT FEW ARE CHOSEN
        REALLY MEANS   ISBN: 978-0-6151-7487-7

HEAVENLY ANGEL LAY LAY AND GUARDIAN ANGEL SHADOW GUESS THE REAL AGE OF THE
        EARTH   ISBN: 978-0-6151-7488-4

AN ABUSED MAN'S BATTLES, TRYING TO PROTECT HIS BOYS   ISBN: 978-0-6151-5191-5

HEAVENLY ANGEL LAY LAY *EXPLAINS WHY* <u>PROFESSIONAL COUNSELORS HAVE 'HARDENED HEARTS'</u>

STRAIGHTEN OUT THE HEART

The following is an excerpt from my book called, **MATTHEW'S WORD 'TWO':REAL WORD OF GOD BIBLE**. This is one of the Bible Mysteries Heavenly Angel Lay Lay shared with me on our way, taking Rachael to the Promised Land. Since a Heavenly Angel told me this, how can I change anything that any Heavenly Angel said and make it better? If you don't know who Heavenly Angel Lay Lay is or how I was allowed to work with three different Heavenly Angels, then you will need to purchase **MATTHEW'S WORD 'TWO':REAL WORD OF GOD BIBLE** and read it (ISBN: 1-4116-6995-9). The first half of **MATTHEW'S WORD 'TWO':REAL WORD OF GOD BIBLE** is about how I was allowed to work with three different Heavenly Angels to begin with. The second half of **MATTHEW'S WORD 'TWO':REAL WORD OF GOD BIBLE** contains about 100 pages of Biblical facts Heavenly Angel Lay Lay was allowed to share with me. You will need to read the whole book in order to understand how I was allowed to work with three different Heavenly Angels for a little over a year of my life. Lay Lay explained to me why Adam didn't stop Eve from eating the 'forbidden fruit', what caused Cain to get so angry he killed Abel, what happened to the Raven from Noah's Ark and why it had to be the Raven that was let out first and then the Dove, how old the Earth really is, along with other Biblical Secrets that theologians and theorists do not know.

Lay Lay said, "As for Paul, there was pain in his heart, the difference between Christians today and Paul is that Paul didn't want to do the sin, even though he couldn't stop. Paul started catching himself doing it out of pure reflex, at times Paul caught himself before he did the sin and was able to stop himself, but Paul strived to be as perfect as he could be in Jesus. Another thing Christians need to remember is that Paul was years into his ministry when God said, 'My <u>Grace</u> is sufficient for thee.' Paul wasn't always that perfect when he first started his ministry, what Paul did acknowledge and a lot of Christians today don't acknowledge is that Paul never tried to hide anything. Paul also kept working diligently in prayer and meditation on those minor sins Paul started out with, and over time

Paul was able to stop all but one minor sin. A lot of Christians use the Crucifixion, Blood, and Resurrection today as a free-ticket to continue to sin, there is a huge difference between the two. God still used Paul to minister and preach the gospel of Jesus, God made a point with Paul so others could see it. Right now you have a few masks on due to the pain in your heart, you are drinking, smoking, and when you start talking very serious you raise your voice and swear at times, being a human male you are probably lusting at times as well, those sins usually go together, they are basically all minor sins. The difference between lusting in your mind like you do at times and lusting in your heart is because you can't control the thoughts that pop into your mind, but you do have the power in choosing whether to act on those thoughts or not, see the difference? The more you read the Word of God the less and less those negative thoughts will come into your mind. You've been beaten on your arms, shoulders, and face with women's fists, you like other Christian men don't go to shelters because shelters are built for women and what man would want to go to a shelter with all women in it? No woman who has been beaten by a man would want to go to a shelter with all men in it. Christian men also realize it's against the Word of God to leave their spouse for that purpose, no Christian can lead their spouse to Jesus as Jesus commands them to when they are in a shelter or when the Christian puts a Restraining Order on their unsaved spouse keeping their spouse away for a year. The Word of God says, 'the saved is **BOUND** to the unsaved except for two Biblical Reasons. One is adultery, the other is if the unsaved chooses to leave the saved. The saved is **BOUND** to the unsaved so that the saved will bring the unsaved to Jesus and inherit the Kingdom of Heaven' as well. If the saved leaves the unsaved for anything other than those two biblical reasons the saved will have to answer to the Father in Heaven on Judgment Day for their 'unsaved spouse's soul' burning in Hell for all eternity. The fact is, if the 'saved' doesn't keep that command the 'saved' is questioning God's wisdom just like Eve did. You've seen woman in court rooms actually lie under oath about what happened and then step outside the courtroom and tell the man they were sorry for lying under oath, but they were advised to from the counselor because the counselors explain to them without a certain testimony the authorities don't have a case. Since there are either no witnesses or witnesses just from their own families and no bruises on the man, the man can't prove anything, society takes the word of the woman over the man which is exactly opposite the Word of God. You understand in your heart what it's like to be a Battered Christian Male, always being discriminated against. Yes, Jesus knows what women have done to you and other men, so does society, they just don't want to admit it. Special Interest Groups pay too much 'soft money' so Congress and the legal system looks the other way, the Laws of the Land are basically made for women and children when it comes to Domestic Relations at this time in your culture, but that's all changing to help the family instead of rewarding the women to stay single and raise their own children. Women are going to be put back in their place, being 'submissive' to their husbands and under men, just like Eve 'blew it' in 'the garden' in Eden, women in your society 'blew it' also, they are no better than Eve and again, Adam was not around. Adam was taken out of the picture through the legal system when it came to raising the children. Eve fell for Satan's deceptive trick wanting to be better than God created her, as a goddess, and women in your society fell for Satan's trap wanting to be more than where God cursed women to be, being 'submissive to their husbands' and under men. All those man made laws that protect the privacy of the women 'sealing the court papers' and 'doctor reports' for the ones who have had affairs and gotten pregnant, choosing to have either abortions or adoptions without the husband or boyfriend even knowing about the abortion or adoption will be opened.   The children, grandchildren, and great grandchildren will need that information to have that 'void' in their hearts filled. Without that 'void' filled, the human really can't love someone else with **ALL** THEIR HEARTS, not even their own spouse or children. Just like Detta, she won't know what REAL LOVE is until she does a lot of crying letting the pain and heartache out of her heart the day she Crosses Over, that's not just due to the demons in her, that's also due to the heartache in her heart.   Abortions and miscarriages are murder when humans induce the miscarriage by some medical means. In the long run, adoptions and foster care do much more harm than they ever did any good. Laws will change for family unity, in order for family peace to exist, Jesus must be the God the family worships, HE IS THE PRINCE OF PEACE, then the husband and wife must be 'one flesh' second, then the children third to make the family ONE UNIT, that means 'sealed court papers' for adoption will be opened, the secular men and women won't like it. That means they will have to stop 'playing around on the side' and tell their own spouses the truth about who they have been with. They haven't been spiritually, physically, or emotionally married to their spouses for years now, just legally married to them. The Christian men and women who are already living by the Word of God and don't have a lot of heartache will love it. Jesus will be able to remove the heartache from the hearts of Christian men and women. The man will have a lot of questions he will want his wife and another man to answer, THE TRUTH WILL COME OUT, because the TRUTH MUST COME OUT, or the children will continue to suffer. When it comes to emotions in the heart, Jesus has to take His time healing the heart, but knowing the 'whole truth' is the foundation for His healing to begin. Christians will need to sit back, watch, and wait, they laid their children on the 'alter' and need to leave them there. It would be a sin for them to pick those burdens back up and get involved while Jesus is still in the process that brings their children back to them, then lead their children to Jesus and teach the children about the Stripes Jesus took for them. Yes, the real parents may see their children, grandchildren, or great grandchildren suffering, but it's better for them to suffer on Earth for a time than in Hell for all eternity, independent women will hate the changes Jesus is going to make in the United States. Jesus is breaking the human's hearts down to get the pain out through their children and the three to four generation curse. He has seen the abominations and lies that have been committed by the parents, grandparents, and great grandparents from the children's Real Physical Bloodline. If the child comes to Christ and the child says a 'half-hearted' or 'stipulated prayer', then Jesus won't come in and the Stripes of Christ won't heal the child,. that will depend on what the parent has taught the child when the child was being raised. If the parent didn't teach the child about Jesus from the King James Version of the Word of God, then the child will suffer more because the child won't be able to accept His stripes as quickly. The submissive Christian women won't have anything to worry about unless they had children before they asked Jesus to be their Lord and Savior and became submissive Christian ladies. Christians sing about Jesus being the Potter, breaking the Vessel and making a New Vessel out of them, and that's what's going to happen. Remember, 'the words you speak is created into existence', whether you mean what you say or not doesn't matter. Those words may take a few years to create something, but the words will create none the less. When something is spoken into existence, there can be no stipulations on how it takes place, just that it will take place. How is up to Jesus, the Father in Heaven, and the Holy Spirit, and how much damage Satan was able to do in the process. As I said before, 'It's always best to tell the whole truth, no matter how bad the truth is. If the whole truth is out in the open to begin with, Satan can't use any of the human's past against them several years down the road, the whole truth is already out. Real parents and children will be united for the first time or reunited and that missing void in their hearts will start healing. The parents who lied to their children will be disowned by their own children, just like Detta found out she was actually a recruit after all those years, she found out her whole life is one big fat lie. That's how Jesus is going to get the negative emotions to flow from the hearts of hardened-hearted, like yourself. Once the whole truth is out, the negative emotions from hurt and heartache can flow, then the positive emotions can go into the heart to heal the heart. Humans think they can go around the Word of the Living God. HIS WORD IS THE SAME, YESTURDAY, TODAY, AND FOREVER. JESUS CHRIST OF NAZARETH IS STILL ON THE THRONE AND STILL IN CONTROL. There are a lot of Single Christian Males just like you, being battered, yet not bruised, beaten up by their wives or girlfriends still longing in their hearts for a Solid Christian Wife and being able to raise their own children. Jesus promised His children He would give them the 'desires of their hearts' if they stood on His Word, Jesus must keep His promise. You and a lot of other Christian men in the United States and in other countries all around the world have had your families taken away through the Laws of the Land which is being operated by Satan. Christian men and women who have followed the Word of God and never denied Him even in private or public places will be blessed with families, good careers, and be able to raise new families according to His Word without any interference from anyone, including family members and the Laws of the Land, if that's what their heart's desires are. Others who have done the same, will be blessed with whatever their Hearts Desires are according to His Word and His Will. Jesus must keep His promise to those who have put Him and His Word FIRST even through persecution. You have HIS PROMISE ON THAT. Humans don't live for several hundred years like they used to in the Old Testament anymore, so in order to keep His promise Jesus is already stepping in and is changing the attitudes and hearts of humans in the United States of America and other countries as well, this will happen in a very short time for Him to keep His promise to ALL HIS CHILDREN, or as you like saying, His Fiancé. Jesus doesn't go by any Church Doctrine, He goes by His Word and His Word alone, Christian's are straightening up and standing up for Jesus and His Word instead of reading those False Doctrine Bibles. Jesus has seen the heartache of all Christians in your society. Your case is not, as a lot of Counselors would call, 'An Isolated Case', there is no such thing as 'An Isolated Case'. Yet even with your minor sins and all the heartache you have, you still made two Power Demons go to Hell, the third Power Demon was just hanging on by his fingernails when he was able to get the phone back on the hook making you loose your connection to the vessel and you did that in less than five minutes. You didn't have to tell the 'unclean spirit', 'I am the Child of the Most High God', he told you. The unclean spirit actually said, 'I know you, you are His Child.', the demons know you are the Child of Jesus, that's why the demons don't want to go to Stanfield, Oregon. The demons know when the vessel gets to Stanfield, Oregon the demons will be commanded to Hell, the demons know you have 'The Power'. If Jesus had to wait for any one of His children to be perfect, without sin in their lives, Jesus would never be able to get anything done because everyone sins in one aspect or another. What Christians keep forgetting is that the Father in Heaven sees a Christian as being 'perfect', because of the Blood of Christ. He sees you through the Crucifixion, Blood, and Resurrection."

I asked, "How do we test the 'fruits on the tree' then?" Lay Lay said, "By what comes out of the Christian's mouth, the words they speak creating things into existence, the actions follow the words, it doesn't matter if they are 'sinning in the flesh' or not, they still have the power to 'speak things into existence' and to 'talk about the good things Jesus has done for them.' Whatever a human speaks through their tongue is created, or they are 'idle words' and will be judged accordingly, that's where the real 'fruits of the tree' are, just because a Christian witnesses to another person, doesn't mean that human will accept Jesus as their Lord and Savior. Whether a human accepts Jesus as their Lord and Savior or not that Christian still has 'good fruits of his work on his tree', that Christian did his job by speaking about Jesus. That's what humans will be judged for, their 'good works' and 'idle words' not how many souls the Christian leads in the Salvation Prayer and into the Kingdom of Heaven, if that were the case, it wouldn't be fair because of Free-Will, a human can be witnessed to for twenty years and not accept Jesus, that's not the fault of the Christian, that's Free-Will. Does that make the Christian have any less 'good fruits on their tree?' No, the fruits are there because of the words spoken into existence through the power of the tongue (witnessing), that's why in the legal system Satan doesn't want Jesus talked about in public meetings, court rooms, schools, or any other place. Satan knows the power of the tongue and that words create things, talking about Jesus would take more souls away from Hell."

I asked, "Why is it so hard to stop smoking, drinking, or cocaine/heroine use, or obesity?" Lay Lay said, "The vessel gets used to the drug in the system, once the demon is off or out and Jesus is in the vessel, and the vessel is Anointed with Oil from Israel and prayed over by two or more Holy Spirit filled Christians, and that Supernatural Covering is over the vessel, then the demon can't latch back on or go back into the vessel unless the vessel itself tells Jesus to leave their heart through their words or actions, like playing with Satan's Play Toys, such as going to a Fortune Teller, playing with a Ouiji Board, or children playing with cartoon toys with the ability to change their shapes from one form to another, or getting their Super Powers from outside sources, those are Satan's Toys as well and the child could actually become possessed with a Friendly Unclean Spirit if the child plays with those toys, even with the Supernatural Covering when the vessel is prayed over and anointed with Oil from Israel if the vessel sins again, the flesh will remember the characteristics of the demon, whether the demon was in the vessel or just attached to the vessel, that's why when someone starts drinking again, or smoking again the human mind and body automatically remembers the vessel used to need that particular drug to function, the vessel goes right back to where the vessel was before, then stopping the habit is up to the human to put the alcohol, cigarette, or cocaine down and the vessel will go through withdrawals getting the drug out of the system again, or to stop having sexual desires, or whatever the sin is. Jesus wants that vessel to prove to Him the vessel will never use the drug or do the sin again. Detta, for instance, will be delivered, but if she is under hypnosis and is taken back to a point in time when she was possessed and someone starts saying the name of 'Jesus Christ of Nazareth' the memory of the demon may manifest itself through her memory because of the time frame the 'subconscious mind' is at through hypnosis, her memory could actually growl or snarl even though the demon is gone.

You have done wonders with Detta and the girls with their 'subconscious mind', when you first started talking to her, she was using the screen name 'MrsBadluck, then it went to DJorDove, then to Dove340, then to Detta, just to name a few, you can see how her self-image has gone up and gotten better, the 'subconscious mind' remembers everything, even the growling and snarling of demons from the past and their characteristics. The 'subconscious mind' doesn't distinguish 'good from evil', it just deals in 'facts, emotions, and Free-Will.' The 'conscious mind' deals with 'good from evil, emotions, and Free-Will.' The 'subconscious mind' is the person's eyes to the Spiritual World where the 'conscious mind' is the person's eyes to the Physical World, that's why Adam was so smart, he was using his 'subconscious and conscious mind combined' before the fall of mankind, the 'conscious and subconscious minds' were both together, the 'tree of good and evil' opened up their physical eyes and separated the 'conscious mind from the subconscious mind', Adam and Eve started using their 'conscious mind' and knew 'Good from Evil.' That's why Satan attacks the 'physical body', it's connected to the 'conscious mind' (good and evil) where the 'subconscious mind' is connected to the Spiritual World,. that's why Jesus had you work on her 'subconscious mind', the source of her problems were stored in the 'subconscious mind', the things the 'conscious mind' has already lived through, that's how her self-image was able to get so much better with just a year of counseling her. Jesus took you to 'the root of her problem' in her 'subconscious mind' and 'spirit' in her heart' and 'her past' in her life."

I asked, "What do you mean, 'the root of the problem'?" Lay Lay said, "Humans aren't drinking, smoking, committing adultery, taking prescription medication or obese for fun,. they aren't sinning just to be sinning,. they are sinning because there is something in their hearts they need to work through and get over, the sins are just the cover-up for the real problem. Some kids start smoking because of 'Peer Pressure.' The real problem is they feel inferior to their friends and smoking is a way to 'fit in', they don't have the self-image to say smoking is wrong. Take a man or woman who gets served 'divorce papers', they start drinking or drinking more heavily. The drinking isn't the real problem; they use the alcohol to cover-up the pain in their heart, the alcohol helps them temporarily not think about the real problem. The drinking to begin with may have been caused by the mate's family not accepting them, drinking is their way to cope with the rejection. They feel they aren't good enough for the man or woman they are in love with because their family, especially mothers, believe their son or daughter can do better. They start drinking a lot more after the divorce papers, separation papers, or restraining orders are filed and their mate leaving them. You have been counseling people who have been divorced and on a second marriage or living with someone. What have the mothers said about the human their son or daughter is married to now compared to the last marriage?" I said, "Well, the most I have noticed is when the mother will come up with a comment like, at least he/she is better than so-and-so." Lay Lay said, "Exactly, the mother is comparing the son or daughter's present mate to the last one, the second mate the mother can live with because she has something to compare the human with. In the first marriage there was no way to compare the mate, so now the mother is content because her son or daughter has someone better, or so she believes, then the mother will stop being so judgmental towards the mate of the son or daughter." I said, "Mothers shouldn't even be comparing mates to begin with, they aren't the ones married to the person." Lay Lay said, "You're right, they shouldn't, but just like Mandy with Rachael, they do. Mandy has stopped Rachael (Detta) from coming to you countless times, you were good enough to get her daughter out of the village, but not good enough to marry her daughter. Mandy is looking at the age difference between Rachael (Detta) and you, thinking my daughter can do better, and not the love you have for Rachael (Detta). Mothers truly do only want the best for their son or daughter, but their short-term thinking isn't sufficient to distinguish what the long-term results will be if their son or daughter stays married to a mate over a long period of time, all the mother can see is the short-term and judges in that respect. There will be a day when Mandy will wish she wouldn't have interfered so much between you and Rachael. Everyone has a mask on, it's finding out what the real problem is that caused them to put the mask on in the first place and working through that problem, that is the real solution to the problem, treating a symptom isn't going to fix any problem.

Women who have been raped will usually go one of three ways. They will either start wearing very tight clothes showing off what they have lost, due to the rape. They figure, 'if a man is going to take me anyway, I may as well show it off and sell it.' The ones who don't go that way will start wearing very loose fitting clothes not letting anyone see their bodies, afraid if they show their bodies off in nice looking clothes, they may get raped again. The ones who do go with the loose fitting clothes sometimes go even farther. They start overeating, putting on weight thinking to themselves, 'If I put on enough weight then no man will want me so I won't have to worry about being raped anymore.', or they will start wearing very high buttoned shirts or blouses, making sure they don't even show off their neck."

ISAAC

AND

REBEKAH

(CONTINUED FROM:
ABRAHAM AND SARAH PART 2 IN
HEAVENLY ANGEL LAY LAY
EXPLAINS
THE BIBLICAL GROUNDS FOR
MARRIAGE,
SEPARATION, AND DIVORCE)

After I tell the reader Biblical Facts that Heavenly Angel Lay Lay told me when I was working with her and Shadow, I will be writing about different stories from the King James Version of the Word of God talking about the family aspects in the Word of God. How the different couples in the bible met, what the couples went through, and what men, women, and children are commanded to do and not to do according to the Word of God. Just like HEAVENLY ANGEL LAY LAY taught me how to do.

ISAAC AND REBEKAH

Genesis 24:1-67
1) And Abraham was old, and well stricken in age: and the LORD had blessed Abraham in all things.
2) And Abraham said unto his eldest servant of his house, that ruled over all that he had, Put, I pray thee, thy hand under my thigh: [The steward of the house is Eliezer of Damascus (Genesis 15:2)]
3) And I will make thee swear by the LORD, the God of heaven, and the God of the earth, that thou shalt not take a wife unto my son of the daughters of the Canaanites [(Abraham is still in Canaan. Isaac and his wife would be 'unequally yoked' and the 'sanctified. Abraham's son, Isaac would be bound to the unsanctified), his wife

who didn't worship the Lord]', among whom I dwell:

    Deuteronomy 7:3

    3) Neither shalt thou (you) make marriages with them; thy (your) daughter thou (you) shalt not give unto his son, nor his daughter shalt thou (you) take unto thy (your) son.

    Joshua 23:12-13

    12) Else if ye (you) do in any wise go back, and cleave (cling) unto the remnant (survivors) of these nations, *even* these that remain (survivors) among you, and shall make marriages with them, and go in unto them, and they to you:

    13) Know for a certainty that the LORD your God will no more drive out *any of* these nations from before you (Will no longer help you); but they shall be snares and traps unto you, and scourges (open wounds) in your sides, and thorns in your eyes, until ye (you) perish from off this good land which the LORD your God hath given you.

    1 Kings 11:2

    2) Of the nations *concerning* which the LORD said unto the children of Israel, Ye (you) shall not go in to them, neither shall they come in unto you: *for* surely they will turn away your heart after their gods (make you true 'backsliders'):   Solomon clave unto these in love (turned to 'false gods').

    Exodus 34:16

    16) And thou (you) take of their daughters unto thy (your) sons, and their daughters go a-whoring after their gods (serving several 'false gods'), and make thy (your) sons go a-whoring after their gods (turning their back on God and serve 'false gods' instead because their daughters serve 'false gods').

4) But thou (you) shalt go unto my country (Ur of Chaldees) , and to my kindred, and take a wife unto (for) my son Isaac.

5) And the servant said unto him (Abraham),

Peradventure the woman will not be willing to follow me unto this land: must I needs bring thy (your) son again unto the land from whence (where) thou camest (Ur, where Abraham was from) (If the woman won't come to Isaac in this new land, should I take Isaac to her)?

6) And Abraham said unto him, Beware thou (you) that thou (you) **bring not my son thither (there) again** [(No, don't take Isaac to her. This was said twice, once here and once in verse 8).

7) The LORD God of heaven, which took me from my father's house, and from the land of my kindred (kin, blood relatives), and which spake unto me, and that sware (promised) unto me, saying, Unto thy seed will I give this land; he shall send his angel before thee (you), and thou shalt take a wife unto my son from thence (there).

8) And if the woman will not be willing to follow thee (you), then thou shalt be clear from this my oath: **only bring not my son thither (there) again** (Do not take Isaac to her. Abraham was so insistent on this issue, Abraham knew God had promised Abraham that Abraham's seed would be too numerous to count)

9) And the servant put his hand under the thigh of Abraham his master, and sware (promised) to him concerning that matter (To bring back a wife for Isaac).

10) And the servant took **ten camels** of the **camels of his master** (Meaning Abraham had many more camels than just ten), and departed; for all the goods of his master were in his hand (The servant took whatever he needed for the trip and loaded all the good on the backs of the camels, nine camels worth of goods. Right now we know the servant had to have at least one camel to ride on. We find out later there are other men that went on the journey with this servant, so we can assume there were nine camels that had men on them along with all the provisions of the journey. By the time they arrived

at their destination all the provisions would have been used up and they would have had to purchase more food and provisions for the journey back): and he arose, and went to Mesopotamia (a country), unto the city of Nahor.

In Genesis 16:3) And Sarai Abram's wife took Hagar her maid the Egyptian, after Abram had dwelt ten years in the land of **Canaan**, and gave her to her husband Abram to be his wife.

(One mile is a unit of linear measure, equal to 1,760 yards or 5,280 feet or 1,609.35 meters, used in the U.S., Great Britain) (Merriam-Webster)

(One kilometer is a unit of length of distance, equal to 1,000 meters or 3,280.8 feet, or about 5/8 of a mile) (Merriam-Webster)

(600 miles x 1,609.35 meters or 1.67 kilometers per one mile = 965,610 meters in 600 miles (Merriam-Webster).

(965,610.35 meters / 1000 meters per one kilometer = 965.61 kilometers)

(1.67 kilometers per one mile)

(0.62 miles per one kilometer)

(25 miles per day travel = 41.75 kilometers per day travel)

[Now we also know the servant's journey started in Hebron, Canaan (We get this from Genesis 23:19)

19) And after this, Abrahah buried sarah his wife in the cave of the field of Machpelah before Mamre: the same is Hebron in the land of Canaan.

From Hebron, Canaan to Nahor, a city in Mesopotamia to get Isaac's wife. Mesopotamia is between the Tigris and Euphrates Rivers in modern day Turkey. The approximate distance between Hebron, Canaan and Nahor, Mesopotamia (I'm going to use Ur instead of Nahor because Ur is actually on a map. It will still give you an idea which is what these figures are supposed to do, just give you an idea of what everyone went through). From Hebron to Damascus is about 160 miles or 167.2 kilometers north and from Damascus to Mari is about 300 miles or 501 kilometers north east and Mari to Ur is about 400 miles or 668 kilometers east. From Hebron to Ur is 160+300+400=860 miles or 167.2+501+668=1,336.2 kilometers north-east

1.67 kilometer=1 mile (Merriam-Webster) The number for the kilometer is higher than the number for the mile. Each camel being weighed down with a very heavy load could carry 450 kg/990 lbs (Merriam-Webster), the camel works only six to eight months of the year (Merriam-Webster), so the journey to her country and back would have had to be during that time period. The rest of the time out of the year, the camel needs to rest and recuperate. A working camel can go about 25 miles or 41.75 kilometers a day (Merriam-Webster). So it took approximately 34.4 days/6 days a week=5.7 weeks to get to Ur from Hebron. We also need to remember they rested on the seventh day, in other words, no one went anywhere on the seventh day, that's why I divide the numbers by six instead of seven. A camel can drink 100 litres/21 gallons of water in ten minutes, which is stored in their bloodstream. Each gallon of water weighs 8 lbs. Each camel could carry 124 gallons of water. If the camels were just carrying their minimum load weight, they wouldn't have been able to carry all the provisions, water, and men that it would have taken to take this journey. We also need to remember that on the journey back there was the bride to be along with all the servants on the camels. So the time of the journey back would have had to have been longer than the time to get to her country to begin with. The servant did leave her family with gifts so some of the weight would have been gone. The tent, cooking stuff, bedding, and other provisions would have still been on the camels, etc. We are looking at least an eight week journey to her country and at least eight weeks back home to get to Isaac]

11) And he (the servant) made his camels to kneel down without (outside of) the city by a well of water at the time of the evening, even the time that women go out to draw water.

12) And he (the servant) said O LORD God of my master Abraham, I pray thee (ask you), send me good speed (quickly) this day, and shew (show) kindness unto my master Abraham.

13) Behold, I stand here by the well of water; and the daughters of the men of the city come out to draw water:

14) And let it come to pass, that the damsel to whom I shall say, Let down thy (your) pitcher, I pray (ask) thee (you), that I may drink; and she shall say, Drink, and I will give thy (your) camels drink also: let the same be she that thou (you) hast (have) appointed for thy (your) servant Isaac; and thereby shall I know that thou (you) hast (have) shewed (shown) kindness unto my master. **(Now, this is very important for all the women today who are praying for husbands and wanting confirmation about the man that Jesus is sending to them. Abraham didn't ask for a sign or a confirmation, Isaac didn't ask for a sign or a confirmation, <u>the servant asked for a sign, but not a confirmation</u>)**

15) And it came to pass, before he had done speaking, that, behold, Rebekah came out, who was born to Bethuel, son of Milcah, the wife of Nahor, Abraham's brother, with her pitcher upon her shoulder.

16) And <u>the damsel was **very fair to look upon**</u> (she was good looking), a virgin, neither had any man known her (Making the point that Rebekah was a virgin twice): and she went down to the well, and filled her pitcher, and came up.

17) And the servant ran to meet her (Rebekah), and said, Let me, I pray thee (ask of you), drink a little water of

thy (from your) pitcher.

18) And she (Rebekah) said, Drink, my lord (the servant): and she hasted (hurried), and let down her pitcher upon her hand, and gave him drink.

19) And when she had done giving him drink, she said, I will draw water for thy (your) camels also, until they (the camels) have done drinking (Now remember how much water even one camel can drink? That's a lot of water. Now here is the sign that the servant wanted, no confirmation was ever given by any third party as so many women today want from Jesus Christ. Did the sign come from the woman's friend, the woman's father or mother, or the woman's brother or sister? No, the sign came from the woman herself because that's who the servant ask the sign to come from and there is no confirmation. Did the woman ask for confirmation? No. There is no where in scriptures that the woman ever asked for any confirmation. Also, this woman knows the value of camels, she offered to give the camels to drink knowing they are very valuable. A good family woman for any man who desires a family, or in their culture with a lot of valuable animals and precious items making sure the assets of this servants master's family is protected).

20) And **she** (Rebekah) **hasted** (She RAN, HURRIED, she knew the camels were very thirsty and they needed lots of water fast), and emptied her pitcher into the trough, and **ran** again unto the well to draw water, and drew for all his camels (The camels were drinking water so fast she had to run to draw water and get enough water back to the trough for all the camels to drink. She had to draw for ten camels and remember how much water each camel can drink and how fast each camel can drink a gallon of water?).

21) And the man wondering at her (watching her) held his peace (didn't say a word), to wit (wondering) whether the LORD had made his journey prosperous or

not (The servant was waiting on the LORD for the answer).

22) And it came to pass, as the camels had done drinking, that the man took a golden earring of half a shekel weight, and two bracelets for her hands of ten shekels weight of gold;

23) And said, Whose daughter art thou (you)? tell me, I pray thee (beg of you): is there room in thy (your) father's house for <u>us</u> (this is the first mention of others with the servant) to lodge in? (Now we know the trip up and back probably took a lot longer, no man or woman can walk or run as fast as a camel and keep it up for hours on end, ever day)

24) And she said unto him, **I am the daughter of Bethuel (Bethuel is the father of Rebekah) the son of Milcah (Milcah is the mother of Bethuel and grandmother of Rebekah), which she bare unto Nahor (Nahor is the father of Bethuel and grandfather of Rebekah. Nahor and Abraham were brothers, both from their father Terah, and Isaac is Abraham's son. Isaac and Bethuel, the father of Rebekah, are first-cousins).**

25) She said moreover unto him, We have both straw and provender (Dry food for domestic animals) (Merriam-Webster) enough, and room to lodge in (God had her go over and above what the servant asked God for to begin with. Going over and above what someone asks God for would make someone nervous and start doubting if the sign really was from God in today's society. They ask God to bless them, then when He does, they wonder if the blessing really is from God to begin with because it's not exactly what they ask for to their specifications, but it is to God's specifications. Remember the servant only asked God to have the woman to draw water for him and the camels as well, nothing to do with food and provisions).

26) And the man bowed down his head, and worshipped

the LORD.

27) And he (the servant) said, Blessed be the LORD God of my master Abraham, who hath not left destitute my master of his mercy and his truth: I being in the way, the LORD led me to the house of my master's brethren.

28) And the damsel ran, and told them of her mother's house (All the people in her mother's house including the servants) these things.

29) And Rebekah had a brother, and his name was Laban: and Laban ran out unto the man, unto the well.

30) And it came to pass, when he (Laban) saw the earring and bracelets upon his sister's hands, and when he heard the words of Rebekah his sister, saying, Thus spake the man unto me; that he came unto the man; and, behold, he stood by the camels at the well (Rebekah's brother didn't even ask for a confirmation, he took the word of Abraham's servant as Rebekah did. Now what woman today is going to do that without confirmation? Yet women keep praying for Jesus to send them a Christian man all the time and wonder why Jesus doesn't answer. Jesus does answer, they aren't listening. That makes me wonder how close the women are to Christ. They need confirmation, and then they want the confirmation to be from someone who isn't even praying to bring a future husband to them. That means they are doubting instead of walking in faith. How many confirmations did Noah have? None. Yet he spent years, maybe even centuries, building the ark with a bright blue, hot, sunny sky over his head).

31) And he said, Come in, thou blessed of the LORD; wherefore standest thou without? for I have prepared the house, and room for the camels (The house is ready for the servant and there is room for the camels in what we would call a barn as well).

32) And the man came into the house: and he ungirded (What we would call taking backpacks and bridles off,

the bridle is the mouth piece with the reigns attached if you didn't know) his camels, and gave straw and provender (food) for the camels, and water to wash his (The servant Abraham sent) feet, and **the men's feet that were with him** (This is the first mention of several men being with the servant on the journey. I seriously doubt they walked that distance, they probably rode. This confirms the camel's loads were pretty close to maximum weight).

33) And there was set meat before him to eat: but he said, I will not eat, until I have told mine errand (The servant wouldn't take part in anything until his business was completed with the brother). And he (the brother) said, Speak on.

34) And he said, I am Abraham's servant.

35) And the LORD hath blessed my master greatly; and he is become great: and he hath given him flocks, and herds, and silver, and gold, and menservants, and maidservants, and camels, and asses.

36) And Sarah my master's wife bare a son to my master when she was old: and unto him hath he given all that he hath.

37) And my master made me swear, saying, Thou shalt not take a wife to my son of the daughters of the Canaanites, in whose land I dwell (Not to have Isaac to be 'unequally yoked'):

38) But thou shalt go unto my father's house, and to my kindred, and take a wife unto my son.

39) And I said unto my master, Peradventure (just in case) the woman will not follow me.

40) And he said unto me, The LORD, before whom I walk, will send his angel with thee, and prosper thy way; and thou shalt take a wife for my son of my kindred, and of my father's house:

41) Then shalt thou (you) be clear from this my oath, when thou comest to my kindred; and if they give not thee one, thou shalt be clear from my oath.

42) And I came this day unto the well, and said, O LORD God of my master Abraham, if now thou do prosper my way which I go:

43) Behold, I stand by the well of water; and it shall come to pass, that when the virgin cometh forth to draw water, and I say to her, Give me, I pray thee, a little water of thy pitcher to drink;

44) And she say to me, Both drink thou, and I will also draw for thy camels: let the same be the woman whom the LORD hath appointed out for my master's son.

45) And <u>before I had done speaking</u> **in mine heart**, behold, Rebekah came forth with her pitcher on her shoulder; and she went down unto the well, and drew water: and I said unto her, Let me drink, I pray thee.

Isaiah 65:24

And it shall come to pass, that **before they call, I will answer**; and **while they are yet speaking, I will hear** (This reminds me of when I asked Jesus to go ahead and 'sanctify Detta through me' so Jesus could protect her when she was kidnapped and taken to Satan World Order Headquarters. He couldn't help her or protect her until I told Him to go ahead and sanctify her through me from my heart. That's in MATTHEW'S WORD 'TWO':REAL WORD OF GOD BIBLE).

46) And she (Rebekah) made haste, and let down her pitcher from her shoulder, and said, Drink, and I will give thy (your) camels drink also: so I drank, and she made the camels drink also.

47) And I asked her (Rebekah), and said, Whose daughter art thou? And she (Rebekah) said, the daughter of Bethuel, Nahor's son, whom Milcah bare unto him: and I put the earring upon her face, and the bracelets upon her hands.

48) And I bowed down my head, and worshipped the LORD, and blessed the LORD God of my master Abraham, which had led me in the right way to take my master's brother's daughter unto his son.

49) And now if ye will deal kindly and truly with my master, tell me: and if not, tell me; that I may turn to the right hand, or to the left (Abraham's servant wants to know if they will let Rebekah go with him to Isaac or not, so the servant will know what to do next).

50) Then Laban and Bethuel answered and said, The thing proceedeth from the LORD: we cannot speak unto thee bad or good (Laban and Bethuel won't go against what God wants to happen, they consent to Rebekah going to Isaac).

51) Behold, Rebekah is before thee (you), take her, and go, and let her (Rebekah) be thy (your) master's son's (Isaac's) wife, as the LORD hath spoken (Even now, no one asked for a confirmation from God).

52) And it came to pass, that, when Abraham's servant heard their words, he worshipped the LORD, bowing himself to the earth.

53) And the servant brought forth jewels of silver, and jewels of gold, and raiment, and gave them to Rebekah: he (the servant) gave also to her (Rebekah's) brother and to her (Rebekah's) mother precious things.

54) And they did eat and drink, he (Abraham's servant) and the men that were with him, and tarried (stayed) all night; and they rose up in the morning, and he (Abraham's servant) said, Send me away unto my master (The servant asking to be excused with Rebekah).

55) And her (Rebekah's) brother and her (Rebekah's) mother said, Let the damsel abide with us a few days, at the least ten; after that she (Rebekah) shall go (Wanting to keep the men around for a few days, possibly to receive more pay for their stay).

56) And he (Abraham's servant) said unto them (Rebekah's mother and brother), Hinder me not (Don't hold me back), seeing the LORD hath prospered my way; send me away that I may go to my master.

57) And they (Rebekah's mother and brother) said, We

will call the damsel, and enquire at her mouth (Actually asking Rebekah what she wished to do. **Rebekah's Free Will**).

58) And they called Rebekah, and said unto her, Wilt thou go with this man? And she said, I will go (With her own Free Will, Rebekah chose to go that very day by herself. Rebekah knew she had a new family and new responsibilities to her new family. Rebekah was looking out for the well-being of her new family instead of her old family. Rebekah also knew if she stayed there, it would cost her and her new family more precious goods. Another point that needs to be made here is that Rebekah knows nothing at all about Isaac. Just like Isaac knows nothing at all about Rebekah, except they were from the same 'Proper Physical Bloodline'. Rebekah is going totally by faith to her future husband at the word of a servant of her future husband's father, not even the servant of her future husband. How many women today would do that even though they keep praying for God to send them Christian men?).

59) And they sent away Rebekah their sister, and her (Rebekah's) nurse, and Abraham's servant, and his men (Now we have more people who are going to be riding on a camel on the journey back to Canaan).

60) And they blessed Rebekah, and said unto her, Thou art our sister, be thou the mother of thousands of millions, and let thy seed possess the gate of those which hate them.

61) And Rebekah arose, and her damsels (Now Rebekah has damsels going with her and not just her nurse), and they rode upon the camels (Some had to walk on their journey back. That slowed them down even more), and followed the man: and the servant took Rebekah, and went his way (now they had at least three weeks of traveling by camel on the journey back home. We also need to remember that now all of Rebekah's damsels

were with her and some of the damsels from Rebekah and servants of Abraham had to have been walking all that distance. That trip back was longer than the trip to Rebekah. Why? They started out in Hebron as was going to Kadesh-Barnea where Isaac lived. For estimation purposes we can use the same numbers from Hebron to Ur, but reverse them, then we will need to add on some more mileage from Hebron to Kadesh-Barnea. From Ur to Mari is about 400 miles or 668 kilometers west, from Mari to Damascus is about 300 miles or 501 kilometers south west, and from Damascus to Hebron is about 160 miles or 167.2 kilometers south.

From Ur to is Hebron 160+300+400=860 miles or 167.2+501+668=1,336.2 kilometers south west. Now we need to add from Hebron to Kadesh-Barnea where Isaac was living at that time is about 75 miles or 125.25 kilometers south.

So let's add that on to the 860 miles we already have. 860 miles+75 miles=935 miles from Ur to Kadesh-Barnea/25 miles per day=37.4 days/6 =6.2 weeks. Remember, 1.67 kilometer=1 mile (Merriam-Webster).

The Round Trip from Hebron to Ur was 860 miles or 1,336.2 kilometers and 860 miles or 1,336.2 from Ur to Hebron + Hebron to Kadesh-Barnea is 75 miles or 125.5 kilometers=860+860+75=1,795 miles or 1.67x1795=2,997.65 kilometers. 1,795miles/25 miles per day=71.8 days/6=11.9 or 12 weeks round trip.

They couldn't travel that fast with people walking now instead of everyone riding camels. My point with all these facts about the camels and all the time involved in the journey is this. What do you think Rebekah was talking to the servants about during that period of time? They could have counted each and every rock or every sand dune and possibly any bugs or animals in the desert. No, Rebekah was asking the servants about Isaac, Abraham, and Sarah the whole time. This is also when the servants told Rebekah about Hagar and Ishmael and what happened to them. By the time Rebekah arrived at her new home and saw Isaac for the first time, she knew everything about him, Isaac's likes, dislikes, favorite foods, favorite past-time, favorite color, favorite clothes, how he would act and re-act in different situations, what pleased him, what made him angry, etc, Rebekah knew Isaac like the back of her hand. She could have told anyone how long it took for Isaac to have breakfast, how to fix his bath water, anything about Isaac, Rebekah knew everything about Isaac before she ever arrived to see him in person and Isaac knew nothing about Rebekah, except she was the wife that God picked out for him. Rebekah knew nothing about Isaac before she left her brother's house and Isaac knew nothing about Rebekah before he married her. The only thing Rebekah knew is that God had set it up and that was out of the mouth of Abraham's servant, not Abraham, not Isaac, but Abraham's servant who asked God for one particular sign about which woman to take back to Isaac, Isaac didn't even know that much. God chose what Abraham requested, a wife from his own family bloodline to keep the 'Proper Physical Bloodline Clean'. If you don't know anything about the 'Proper Physical Bloodline', then you need to purchase my book called 'MATTHEW'S WORD 'TWO':REAL WORD OF GOD BIBLE and read it, there is a whole section about the Spiritual Bloodline and Physical Bloodline. All this happened without even one confirmation).

62) And Isaac came from the way of the well Lahairoi; for he dwelt in the **south country,** (in Canaan).

63) And Isaac went out to meditate (pray) in the field at the eventide (noon): and he lifted up his eyes, and saw, and, behold, the camels were coming.

64) And Rebekah lifted up her eyes, and when she saw Isaac, she lighted off the camel.

65) For she had said unto the servant, What man is this that walketh in the field to meet us? And the servant had said, It is my master: therefore she took a vail, and covered herself (As soon as she knew the man in the field was Isaac, she covered her face with a vail and jumped off the camel).

66) And the servant told Isaac all things that he had done.

67) And Isaac brought her (Rebekah) into his mother Sarah's tent (<u>Sarah was in the **south country** with Isaac, in Canaan</u>) and took (laid with, made love to) Rebekah, and she became his wife (Nothing else was required to have a marriage); and he loved her: and Isaac was comforted (by Rebekah) after his mother's death. (Sarah, Isaac's mother had been dead for three years now)

Genesis 25:20-34

20) And Isaac was forty years old when he took Rebekah to wife, the daughter of Bethuel the Syrian of Padanaram, the sister to Laban the Syrian.

21) And Isaac intreated (variation of entreat: to plead with especially in order to persuade: ask urgently) (Merriam-Webster) the LORD for his wife, because she (Rebekah) was barren (couldn't conceive. Sounds like Sarai when she was barren): and the LORD was intreated (Variation of entreat: to plead with especially in order to persuade: ask urgently) (Merriam-Webster) of him, and Rebekah his wife conceived.

22) And the children struggled together within her; and she said, If it be so, why am I thus? And she went to enquire (ask) of the LORD.

23) And the LORD said unto her, Two nations are in thy womb, and two manner of people shall be separated from thy bowels (interior parts) (Merriam-Webster); and the one people shall be stronger than the other people; and the elder shall serve the younger (the future being

foretold).

24) And when her days to be delivered were fulfilled (she gave birth), behold, there were twins in her womb.

25) And the first came out red, all over like an hairy garment; and they called his name Esau.

26) And after that came his brother out, and his hand took hold on Esau's heel (The two brothers are already fighting between each other); and his name was called Jacob: and <u>Isaac was threescore years old (sixty)</u> when she (Rebekah) bare them.

27) And the boys grew: and Esau was a cunning hunter, a man of the field; and Jacob was a plain man, dwelling in tents.

28) And Isaac loved Esau, because he did eat of his venison: but Rebekah loved Jacob (This is not good, each parent having a favorite child. Each child should be loved equally by both parent).

29) And Jacob sod pottage (Made vegetable beef soup): and Esau came from the field, and he was faint:

30) And Esau said to Jacob, Feed me, I pray thee, with that same red pottage; for I am faint: therefore was his name called Edom (Esau's name is changed to Edom).

31) And Jacob said, Sell me this day thy birthright (Their offspring are still fighting each other to this very day).

32) And Esau said, Behold, I am at the point to die: and what profit shall this birthright do to me? (Sounds like Christians selling their Heavenly Birthright by denying Christ in public and private meetings so they can receive Government Assistance of one type or another)

33) And Jacob said, Swear to me this day; and he (Esau) sware unto him (Jacob): and he (Esau) sold his birthright unto Jacob (I've actually had to use this scripture filling out United States and county government grievance forms complaining that governmental agencies wanted me to deny Christ to take part in government programs. Of course I refused to

deny Christ, but I wasn't allowed to participate in the government programs either. The governmental agency wanted me to sell my Heavenly Birthright for their help in their governmental program. Denying Christ is selling your Heavenly Birthright. We deny Christ in front of man, Christ will deny us in front of the Angels in Heaven and the Father in Heaven. More about this subject in my book called, 'WHAT'S WRONG WITH THIS PICTURE?' that will be out within the next year. I have to learn how to use some more programs on this computer in order to write that book. There will be a lot of legal papers and a picture of me covered in my own blood after I was beaten by an old girlfriend on the cover).

34) Then Jacob gave Esau bread and pottage (soup) of lentiles (Edible plants, vegetable beef soup); and he (Esau) did eat and drink, and rose up, and went his way: thus Esau despised his birthright (If I would have accepted the governmental agencies proposal to leave Jesus outside the meetings then I would have sold my birthright for the same bowl of pottage).

Genesis 26:1-35

1) And there was a famine in the land, beside the first famine that was in the days of Abraham. And Isaac went unto Abimelech king of the Philistines unto Gerar. (Kadesh-Barnea to Gerar is about 55 miles or 91.85 kilometers north-west/25 miles a day=2.2 days)

2) And the LORD appeared unto him, and said, Go not down into Egypt; dwell in the land which I shall tell thee of:

3) Sojourn in this land (Gerar), and I will be with thee, (Here is another stipulation of God being with us and blessing us. We do as He says and He is with us and bless us, we don't do as He says and we are on our own because He can't protect us any longer, that's our free-will) and will bless thee; for unto thee, and unto thy

seed, I will give all these countries, and <u>I will perform the oath which I sware unto Abraham thy father</u> (Here again God says it's because of Abraham, the prophet, that all this is done for Isaac. Isaac and Ishmael were never Prophets, Abraham was);

4) And I will make thy (your) seed (offspring) to multiply as the stars of heaven, and will give unto thy seed (your offspring) all these countries; and in thy seed (your offspring) shall all the nations of the earth be blessed;

5) Because that Abraham obeyed my voice, and kept my charge, my commandments, my statutes, and my laws. (A lot of Christians don't keep his commandments or statutes, or laws anymore, then they wonder why Christ doesn't bless them. That's why, because they don't do as He commands)

6) And **Isaac dwelt in Gerar**:

7) And the men of the place asked him (Isaac) of his wife (Rebekah); and he (Isaac) said, She is my sister: for he feared to say, She is my wife; lest, said he, the men of the place should kill me for Rebekah; because she was fair to look upon (Isaac lied just like his dad, Abram).

8) And it came to pass, when he had been there a long time, that Abimelech king of the Philistines looked out at a window, and saw, and, behold, Isaac was sporting (flirting, passionately kissing on her, possibly touching her as a husband would and not a brother) with Rebekah his wife.

9) And Abimelech called Isaac, and said, Behold, **of a surety she is thy wife** (Yep, Abraham was definitely **showing** Rebekah was his wife and not his sister); and how saidst thou, She is my sister? And Isaac said unto him, Because I said, Lest I die for her.

10) And Abimelech said, What is this thou hast done unto us? one of the people might lightly have lien with thy wife, and thou shouldest have brought guiltiness upon us (**Laying with someone's husband or wife is a**

very wicked thing to do and curses fall upon those who do it. Those curses are still active today).

11) And Abimelech charged all his people, saying, **He that toucheth this man or his wife shall surely be put to death** (The penalty of Adultery is DEATH. Adultery is not to be taken lightly).

12) Then Isaac sowed (Put forth the effort) in that land, and **received** (Hey, everyone, this is after all the business expenses and taxes are taken out) **in the same year an hundredfold: and the LORD blessed him**.

13) And the man (Isaac) waxed (Easily changed) great, and went forward, and grew (In God) until he became very great (Isaac was willing to be changed by God and molded into what God wanted him to become):

14) For he had possession of flocks, and possession of herds, and great store of servants: and the Philistines envied him.

15) For all the wells which his father's servants had digged in the days of Abraham his father, the Philistines had stopped them, and filled them with earth (Sounds like the Philistines were jealous of Isaac and Abraham too).

16) And Abimelech said unto Isaac, Go from us; for thou art much mightier than we.

17) And Isaac departed thence, and pitched his tent in the valley of Gerar, and dwelt there. (Gerar and the valley of Gerar are two different places, but close to each other. In Verse 6 Isaac and Rebekah were in Gerar, now they are in the valley of Gerar)

18) And Isaac digged again the wells of water, which they had digged in the days of Abraham his father; for the Philistines had stopped them after the death of Abraham: and he called their names after the names by which his father had called them (Digging wells that were already there at one time. There must have been some kind of markers or something to pin-point the wells).

19) And Isaac's servants digged in the valley, and found there a well of springing water.

20) And the herdmen of Gerar (See, Gerar and the valley of Gerar are very close to each other) did strive with Isaac's herdmen, saying, The water is ours: and he called the name of the well Esek; because they strove (fought) with him.

21) And they digged another well, and strove (fought) for that also: and he called the name of it Sitnah.

22) And he removed from thence, and digged another well; and for that they strove not (Didn't fight this time. It took three times to settle down, moved twice): and he called the name of it Rehoboth; and he said, For now the LORD hath made room for us, and we shall be fruitful in the land.

23) And **he (Isaac) went up from thence (there) to Beersheba**. (From Gerar to Beersheba is about 20 miles or 33.4 kilometers south-east/25 miles per day=0.8 of a day)

24) And the LORD appeared unto him (Isaac) the same night, and said, I am the God of Abraham thy father: fear not, for I am with thee, and **will bless thee, and multiply thy seed** <u>for my servant Abraham's sake</u> (Again, this proves Isaac and Ishmael were never prophets, God is keeping His promise to Abraham, not to Isaac or Ishmael. If anyone is wondering why I keep bringing up the fact that Isaac or Ishmael were never prophets, it's because from what I understand, Islam is founded on the prophet Ishmael and Muslim is a branch off Islam, so if there was never a prophet Ishmael to begin with, then there can not be a Heavenly religion of Islam or Muslim, they both stem from a 'Religious Unclean Spirit' that made Ishmael a 'wild man' to begin with, remember Ishmael married an 'Idol Worshipper', from Egypt and dwelt as a 'wild man' in the Wilderness of Paran. Just like the man who came to Jesus with the 'Legion' in him was a 'wild man', remember? Jesus

commanded the 'Legion' into the swine?).

25) And he builded an altar there, and called upon the name of the LORD, and pitched his tent there: and there Isaac's servants digged a well.

26) Then Abimelech went to him from Gerar, and Ahuzzath one of his friends, and Phichol the chief captain of his army.

27) And Isaac said unto them, Wherefore come ye to me, seeing ye hate me, and have sent me away from you?

28) And they said, We saw certainly that the LORD was with thee: and we said, Let there be now an oath betwixt (between) us, even betwixt (between) us and thee (you), and let us make a covenant with thee (you); (Now Abimelech wants to kiss and make up seeing is proof that God is with Isaac, everyone wants a blessing. Talk about the same thing happening today. No one wants anything to do with you until they see with their own eyes that Jesus Christ of Nazareth is on your side, then everyone wants a part of it. Having peace is one thing, being a part of the 'blessings from Jesus' must be learned and lived on an individual basis).

29) That thou wilt do us no hurt, as we have not touched thee, <u>and as we have done unto thee nothing but good</u> (This leaves a lot of room, nothing but good? What about the times Isaac had to re-dig all the wells that Abraham dug in the beginning and they were still kicked out after Abimelech gave them permission to stay on his land. Sounds like they want that kind of good to be done to them), and have sent thee away in peace (Isaac did sent them away in peace, but that's all they got): thou art now the blessed of the LORD.

30) And he made them a feast, and they did eat and drink.

31) And they rose up betimes in the morning, and sware one to another: and Isaac sent them away, and they departed from him in peace.

32) And it came to pass the same day, that Isaac's servants came, and told him concerning the well which they had digged, and said unto him, We have found water.

33) And he (Isaac) called it Shebah: therefore the name of the city is **Beersheba** unto this day.

34) And Esau was forty years old when he took to wife Judith the daughter of Beeri the Hittite (The same tribe who Abraham went to for Sarah's burial place), and Bashemath the daughter of Elon the Hittite (Esau was still angry and became 'unequally yoked' with a woman outside the 'Proper Physical Bloodline', that make her outside the 'Proper Spiritual Bloodline' as well. That's why it was a 'grief of mind' to Isaac and Rebekah): (Esau married out of the 'Proper Physical Bloodline' before Jacob and Rebekah tricked Isaac for Isaac to bless Jacob instead of Esau even though Esau is the oldest son)

35) Which were a grief of mind unto Isaac and to Rebekah. (Esau and Judith are 'Unequally Yoked', they don't fit well together in the marriage bond to each other)

Genesis 27:1-46

1) And it came to pass, that when Isaac was old, and his eyes were dim, so that he could not see, he called Esau his eldest son, and said unto him (Esau), My son: and he (Esau) said unto him (Isaac), Behold, here am I.

2) And he (Isaac) said, Behold now, I am old, I know not the day of my death:

3) Now therefore take, I pray thee, thy weapons, thy (your) quiver and thy (your) bow, and go out to the field, and take me some venison (meat);

4) And make me savoury meat, such as I love, and bring it to me, that I may eat; that my soul may bless thee before I die.

5) And Rebekah heard when Isaac spake to Esau his

son. And Esau went to the field to hunt for venison, and to bring it.

6) And Rebekah spake unto Jacob her son, saying, Behold, I heard thy father speak unto Esau thy brother, saying,

7) Bring me venison, and make me savoury meat, that I may eat, and bless thee before the LORD before my death.

8) Now therefore, my son, obey my voice according to that which I command thee.

9) Go now to the flock, and fetch me from thence two good kids of the goats; and I will make them savoury meat for thy father, such as he loveth:

10) And thou (Jacob) shalt bring it to thy (your) father (Isaac), that he (Isaac) may eat, and that he (Isaac) may bless thee (Jacob) before his (Isaac's) death. (Now why is Rebekah deceiving Isaac, her husband to begin with? I believe I know her reasoning behind her actions, but deception is not the answer. You need to remember Esau is already unequally yoked to Judith, what good would God's blessing be to someone who is not in the 'Proper Physical Bloodline' as Isaac, Rebekah, Esau, and Jacob? Rebekah should have gone and talked to Isaac and reasoned with Isaac about which son to bless with all that God had blessed them with, not falling to a deceptive trick like she did)

11) And Jacob said to Rebekah his mother, Behold, Esau my brother is a hairy man, and I am a smooth man:

12) My father peradventure will feel me, and I shall seem to him as a deceiver; and <u>I shall bring **a curse upon me**</u> (Heavenly Angel Lay Lay said a Christian could curse a human with their faith and the power of their tongue speaking things into existence, here is proof. Christians can have curses put on them by themselves or other Christians), and not a blessing.

13) And his mother (Rebekah) said unto him (Jacob), Upon me (Rebekah) be thy (Jacob's) curse (Here is

proof that a course can go to the parent instead of the child and from the parent to the child, the 'Physical Bloodline' that Heavenly Angel Lay Lay was talking about. This is also found in the New Testament in Matthew 27:25 Then answered all the people and said, His blood *be* on us, and on our children. The curse was cast even though Jesus later said 'forgive them, for they know not what they do.' The curse was still cast earlier and now as Heavenly Angel Lay Lay said, 'Just like the Israelites, the judgment and forgiveness is on an individual basis and not as a family, or a nation), my son: only obey my voice, and go fetch me them (the things I asked for).

14) And he (Jacob) went, and fetched, and brought them (the items) to his mother: and his mother made savoury meat, such as his father loved.

15) And Rebekah took goodly raiment (good clothes) of her eldest son Esau, which were with her in the house, and put them upon Jacob her younger son:

16) And she (Rebekah) put the skins of the kids of the goats upon his hands, and upon the smooth of his neck (being deceptive):

17) And she (Rebekah) gave the savoury meat and the bread, which she had prepared, into the hand of her son Jacob.

18) And he (Jacob) came unto his father, and said, My father: and he said, Here am I; who art thou, my son?

19) And Jacob said unto his father, I am Esau thy first born (deceiving Isaac due to the wish of Rebekah, his mother); I have done according as thou badest me: arise, I pray thee, sit and eat of my venison, that thy soul may bless me.

20) And Isaac said unto his son, How is it that thou hast found it so quickly, my son? And he said, Because the LORD thy God brought it to me (Jacob lying to Isaac, his father, due to the wish of Rebekah, his mother).

21) And Isaac said unto Jacob, Come near, I pray thee,

that I may feel thee, my son, whether thou be my very
son Esau or not (Isaac is doubting, but can't prove
anything).

22) And Jacob went near unto Isaac his father; and he
felt him, and said, The voice is Jacob's voice, but the
hands are the hands of Esau (again deceiving Isaac due
to the wishes of Rebekah, his mother).

23) And he (Isaac) discerned him (Jacob) not, because
his (Jacob's) hands were hairy, as his brother Esau's
hands: so he (Isaac) blessed him (Jacob instead of
Esau).

24) And he said, Art thou my very son Esau? And he
said, I am (Jacob lying to his father, Isaac, due to the
wishes of his mother, Rebekah).

25) And he (Isaac) said, Bring it (the food) near to me,
and I will eat of my son's venison, that my soul (Isaac's)
may bless thee (Jacob instead of Esau). And he (Jacob)
brought it (the food) near to him (Isaac), and he (Isaac)
did eat: and he (Jacob) brought him (Isaac) wine and he
(Isaac) drank.

26) And his father Isaac said unto him, Come near now,
and kiss me, my son.

27) And he (Jacob) came near, and kissed him (Isaac):
and he (Isaac) smelled the smell of his (Esau's clothes
on Jacob) raiment, and blessed him (Jacob), and said,
See, the smell of my son is as the smell of a field which
the LORD hath blessed:

28) Therefore God give thee of the dew of heaven, and
the fatness of the earth, and plenty of corn and wine:

29) Let people serve thee, and nations bow down to
thee: be lord over thy brethren, and let thy mother's
sons (Now this is interesting, every son or daughter was
considered the parents, grandparents, and great
grandparents, until the fourth generation back, it says
mother's sons) bow down to thee: cursed be every one
that curseth thee, and blessed be he that blesseth thee
(Satan can sure work evil when the two parents are

working against each other, and he is still doing evil between the husband and wife today).

30) And it came to pass, as soon as Isaac had made an end of blessing Jacob, and Jacob was yet scarce gone (had barely left) out from the presence of Isaac his father, that Esau his brother came in from his hunting.

31) And he (Esau) also had made savoury meat, and brought it unto his father, and said unto his father, Let my father arise, and eat of his son's venison, that thy soul may bless me.

32) And Isaac his father said unto him, Who art thou? And he said, I am thy son, thy firstborn Esau (Esau being honest).

33) And Isaac trembled very exceedingly, and said, Who? where is he that hath taken venison, and brought it me, and I have eaten of all before thou camest, and have blessed him? yea, and he shall be blessed (Isaac realizing the deception of Rebekah and Jacob's scheme against Isaac and Esau).

34) And when Esau heard the words of his father, he cried with a great and exceeding bitter cry, and said unto his father, Bless me, even me also, O my father.

35) And he said, Thy (your) brother came with subtilty (Satan at work again, using trickery, being deceptive), and hath taken away thy blessing. (Does the 'ends' justify the 'means'? Never, there are always repercussions and side effects of the 'means' to get to the 'ends'. Everything needs to be done properly and in order or there are always drastic results)

36) And he (Jacob) said, Is not he rightly named Jacob? for he hath supplanted me these two times (To take the place of and serve as a substitute for especially by reason of superior excellence or power) (Merriam-Webster): he took away my birthright; and, behold, now he hath taken away my blessing. And he (Esau) said, Hast thou (Isaac, his father) not reserved a blessing for me?

37) And Isaac answered and said unto Esau, Behold, I have made him (Jacob) thy lord, and all his brethren have I given to him for servants; and with corn and wine have I sustained him: and what shall I do now unto thee, my son (Isaac is wondering what to do in this situation)?

38) And Esau said unto his father, Hast thou but one blessing, my father? bless me, even me also, O my father. And Esau lifted up his voice, and wept.

39) And Isaac his father answered and said unto him, Behold, thy dwelling shall be the fatness of the earth, and of the dew of heaven from above;

40) And by thy sword shalt thou live, and shalt serve thy brother; and it shall come to pass when thou shalt have the dominion, that thou shalt break his (Jacob's) yoke from off thy (Esau's) neck (In other words, the time will come that Esau will break away from Jacob's power).

41) And Esau hated Jacob because of the blessing wherewith his father blessed him: and Esau said in his heart, The days of mourning for my father are at hand (Isaac is dieing); then will I slay my brother Jacob (Esau's wrath against Jacob is born and Rebekah started the trickery).

42) And these words of Esau her elder son were told to Rebekah: and she sent and called Jacob her younger son, and said unto him, Behold, thy brother Esau, as touching thee, doth comfort himself, purposing to kill thee (Esau planning to kill Jacob after Isaac's funeral).

43) Now therefore, my son, obey my voice; arise, flee thou to Laban my brother to Haran (Rebekah is sending Jacob to her brother for a time, so Esau can cool off);

44) And tarry (stay) with him a few days (A few days turns out to be 20 years), until thy brother's fury turn away;

45) Until thy (your) brother's anger turn away from thee (you), and he (Esau) forget that which thou (Jacob) hast done to him (Esau): then I will send, and fetch thee (Jacob) from thence (my brother's place): why should I

be deprived also of you both in one day (Because she allowed Satan to bring all this on, not only herself, but also on Isaac, her husband and her two sons as well, with her deception just because she liked one son more than the other.   A mother's short-term motherly thinking. Rebekah is thinking Esau will settle down in a few day? Not even close. A man's wrath is long-term, just like his long-term thinking is long-term)?

46) And Rebekah said to Isaac, I am weary of my life because of the daughters of Heth: if Jacob take a wife of the daughters of Heth, such as these which are of the daughters of the land, what good shall my life do me (Rebekah is still scheming, having second thoughts about what she did, realizing what the consequences are now because of her deception, after the fact, when it's too late. Rebekah is still scheming to get Jacob away from Esau for a few days, having Isaac send Jacob away to her brothers for a wife)?

(CONTINUED IN;
HEAVENLY ANGEL LAY LAY EXPLAINS
THE DIFFERENCE BETWEEN A 'COLD CHRISTIAN' AND A 'BACKSLIDER')

HARDENED

HEARTS

BIBLIOGRAPHY

BIBLIOGRAPHY

1. Merriam Webster's Collegiate Dictionary Tenth Edition (1993), United States of America.

2. The Holy Bible King James Version (1998), B. B. Kirkbride Bible Co., Inc. Indianapolis, IN..USA